I feel...

 happy	 calm	 sad	 angry	 worried	 confident
 scared	 surprised	 disgusted	 unsure	 excited	 embarrassed
 panicked	 focused	 disappointed	 silly	 friendly	 jealous
 bored	 muddled	 tired	 unwell	 hungry	 hot or cold

How do I say "I feel happy" in Makaton?

I feel

Take one hand with your thumb and middle finger pointing to your face and lift your hand up and say, "I feel".

happy.

With a happy look on your face, cup your hands with your palms together and make two gentle swoops and say, "happy".

ISBN 978-1-78270-690-8

Copyright © Channon Gray

All rights reserved. No part of this publication may be reproduced or utilised in any form or by any means electronic or mechanical, including photocopying, recording, or by any information storage and retrieval system now known or hereafter invented, without the prior written permission of the publisher and copyright holder.

No part of this book may be used or reproduced in any manner for the purpose of training artificial intelligence technologies or systems. In accordance with Article 4(3) of the DSM Directive 2019/790, Award Publications limited expressly reserves this work from the text and data mining exception.

First published 2026

Published by Award Publications limited
The Old Riding School, Welbeck, Worksop, S80 3LR

awardpublications @award.books
www.awardpublications.co.uk

25-1206 1

Printed in China

All About Happy Scribble

Written and illustrated by
Channon Gray

award

Happiness means a smile sits beaming on your face.

It feels golden, like the sun, brightening every place.

Feeling happy is fun and everything's just right.

It feels relaxing, comfortable and full of delight.

Ahh! I am Calm Scribble.

Wahoo! I am Happy Scribble.

Happiness grows when we play with our friends or family.

Just being together can fill us with such glee.

At times, it can feel like a star, brightly glowing.

At others,

    like friends cheering us on and keeping us going.

Being happy feels and looks different for everyone.

It might make
you want to

laugh,

giggle,

cheer

and

have fun.

Happiness can feel like a **tickle** in your belly or a **glow** in your heart, like a smile that **stretches** so wide, or a burst of joy — that is the best part!

Did you know that a smile can be catching?

Aww! I am Kindness Scribble.

Sob, sob! I am Sad Scribble.

Smile at someone blue and your faces end up matching!

Feeling happy inside can help others and spread kindness.

When we are happy, we glow with positivity and brightness.

When happiness spreads through our body, we have lots of energy.

We may **sing,** **run,**

If feeling happy seems hard, focus on feeling grateful for what makes you smile.

Take a moment every day to think about all the little things that make life worthwhile.

Let's point our minds in a new direction! I am Direction Scribble.

Maybe it's time
with your friends,

playing outside

or going on
adventures galore.

What are YOU most grateful for?

dance and shake.

Remember, moving our body makes us feel good and awake!

Laughing helps our brain to feel happy, even if things seem bleak –

a giggle with friends, telling a joke, laughing till you're unable to speak!

This is our brain getting busy,
	making **serotonin,** so we feel ace.

It works in the background to lift up our mood,
and keep a smile on our face.

We also need to be kind to ourselves

and recognise how amazing we are.

Self-love fills us with happiness,

like a rainbow filling a jar.

When we are finding something tricky and our BIG feelings are bubbling up,

we can think of the things that make us feel good, and fill up our happy cup.

A **'Happy Map'** plots out a path,
of the things we enjoy
and find fun.

What would your route to happiness be?
It's not the same for everyone!

If we feel worried or sad,
we can think of our **'Happy Place'**
to help us feel glad.

Uhh! I am
Worried Scribble.

It could be a calming and comfortable space...

...or one filled with joyful memories – a wonderful place.

Happiness helps us to beam and glow.

It spreads to everyone around us, helping love and joy grow.

Sometimes, happiness shines like the sun in a cloudless, clear blue sky.

Other times, storm clouds can block out its light, but it's always there, wanting to say, "Hi!"

Feeling happy may come and go –
some days it shines, some days not so.

But, happy **can** be found if you take time to seek.

Happy Scribble Activities

Write or draw happy moments on slips of paper. Pop them into a 'Happy Jar' to help you remember them whenever you need.

Create a 'Happy Album' with photos or drawing of things that make you feel happy. Look at it when you need a happiness boost.

Make a 'Happy and Kind' paper chain. Write or draw an act of kindness, like smiling at a friend, on each link.

The Scribbles Crew love to see your creations! Ask your grown-ups to share them on social media using #TheScribblesCrew

Scan the QR code on the back cover for more great Scribbles Crew activities, sing-along songs and teaching resources specially created by The Exciting Teacher.

www.thescribblescrew.com